I AM
SIMPLE

Balboa Press books may be ordered through booksellers or by contacting:

Balboa Press
A Division of Hay House
1663 Liberty Drive
Bloomington, IN 47403
www.balboapress.com
1 (877) 407-4847

Because of the dynamic nature of the Internet, any web addresses or links contained in this book may have changed since publication and may no longer be valid. The views expressed in this work are solely those of the author and do not necessarily reflect the views of the publisher, and the publisher hereby disclaims any responsibility for them.

ISBN: 978-1-9822-2498-1 (sc)
ISBN: 978-1-9822-2497-4 (e)

Library of Congress Control Number: 2019903747

Print information available on the last page.

Balboa Press rev. date: 03/31/2019

BALBOA.
PRESS
A DIVISION OF HAY HOUSE

I AM SIMPLE

JOY LOVE

When was the last time you did something simple like blow soap bubbles?

That is simple.

As the bubble lets go of the wand it is
no longer in the hands of its creator

but subject to the whims of
a place it knows not.
It is simple.

Moving up and down, to and fro on

the currents, subject to outside forces but always free to move! It Is Simple.

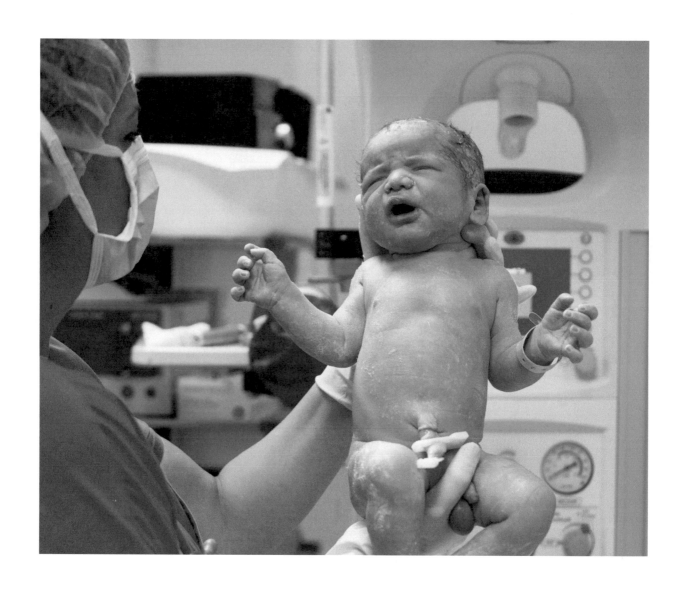

From the moment I enter
I am subject to outside forces;
Moving up and down, to and fro in a
place I know not, always free to move.
I Am Simple.

Bubbles whole and complete
moving, swirling, caught up in
currents in a place they know not!

Life whole and complete moving, swirling,
caught up in currents in a place it knows not!

Can I believe my eyes
What do I see!
Am I a tree?

It appears
I am a tree.

It appears now that I'm a house.

In this place I know not.

Silly me I'm not a tree or a house.

I must be reflecting something outside of me in this place I know not.

**Too complex to be me.
I Am Simple!**

Can I believe my eyes
What do I see!
Am I a girl?

It appears
I am a girl.

Silly me I'm not a girl, or a boy or a group -
I must be reflecting something outside of me
in this place I know not.

I am not a girl.
I Am Simple!

Goodness me
What's happening now!

Am I the colors that seem to
be swirling all over me?
No, this can't be.
I Am Simple!
I am not the feelings swirling all over me –
One moment happy
the next sad.
You can't even see them –
Are they not physical?
Am I not physical?

I know I am not my feelings -
too complex to be me.

I Am Simple!

Some appear large –
Some appear small.

Same but different
How can that be.
Too complex for me to be.
I Am Simple!

I am not my shape nor form.
I am not complex feelings.
I am not my reflections.
I am not my emotions.
All too complex to be me.

I Am Simple.

Now what's happening in this place I know not.

Droplets fall to the earth,
And poof, my outside is discarded
and all that is left, just
like YOU and ME, is

the
Simple Breath
of our Creator!

I am SIMPLE!

About the Author

She is a "Grandma Moses" so to speak, as she waited seventy-three years to write this first book. She believes she has learned much in her lifetime but the most she learned is expressed in this book. Life is much more profound but simpler than one cares to think.

Printed in the United States
By Bookmasters